509

TALL TALES OF ESSEX

by

Dicky Howett

The BBC Essex Al

CW01623104

East Anglian Publishing

Artwork and text © Dicky Howett 1987

All rights reserved. No part of this publication may be reproduced, stored in a retrieval system, or transmitted, in any form, or by any means, electronic, mechanical, photocopying, recording or otherwise, without the prior permission of the publishers.

ISBN 0 900227 83 4

East Anglian Magazine Publishing Limited
Duke Street, Ipswich, IP3 OAJ

Printed in England
Printed by The Five Castles Press, Ipswich

For hornswogglers everywhere

Also by Dicky Howett (with Tim Quinn)
THE DOCTOR WHO FUN BOOK Target Books

Introduction

MY highly popular (according to me) series of Tall Tales on BBC Essex prompted programme presenter Mark Thomas to suggest that I might turn them into a book. That particular conjuring trick now lies (in more ways than one) before you.

I have greatly expanded some of my radio scripts to fill the space available and to boldly go where no man has gone before (at least in Essex). Other items in this book are brand new.

I would however, like to point out that there is nothing parochial or obscure about this book, and although it is Essex based it is offered without prejudice to those of you who are unlucky enough *not* to live in God's Wonderful County.

So take heart Surrey, Buckinghamshire, Merioneth, Durham and Caithness (to name but five), it might be *your* turn next!

But let me tell you a tale.

At the fag-end of World War Two, at a place called Ardleigh Green which is quite near Romford in Essex, a V.2 rocket landed without warning and demolished a street full of houses. In one of these houses a young mother and baby were asleep in a chair. The chair had a very high back to it and the blast from the V.2 rocket pushed the chair over in such a way as to protect mother and child from the crushing weight of the house as it came crashing down on top of them. Fortunately, mother and child were dug out, alive, dusty and quite well.

Forty two years later, that very same child went on to write this book. A book that even Adolf Hitler couldn't stop!

The rest, as they say, is history?

Dicky Howett

BORN in Upminster Essex as early as 1944, Dicky Howett's cartoon creations have enlivened the pages of publications world-wide since 1962. From *'Supermum'* to *'Movie Millie'*, *'Jet Lagg'* to *'Dr. Who?'* plus a whole host of illustrations and humorous drawings for national newspapers and magazines.

This is Dicky's second book. The first, *'The Doctor Who Fun Book'* (with writer Tim Quinn) (Target Books) is currently a best seller throughout the English speaking world.

'Tall Tales Of Essex' is a continuing series, broadcast regularly each month on BBC Essex (throughout the Essex speaking world.)

Dicky is married, has two daughters, lives in Chelmsford and has a train-set in the loft. Despite all that, he still manages to raise a smile.

A Quite Short History of Essex

Some Important Dates

63 BC	Essex established as a settlement by the Danes.
64 BC	Essex re-established due to cracks caused by settlement.
1 BC	Egyptians open the first Pyramid Selling operation in Essex.
½ BC	Pyramids are a flop in Essex due to planning permission being refused for any building over three feet tall.
19 AD	King Sylvia decrees that anyone laughing at his name will be deported to Canvey Island.
20 AD	The whole of Essex is deported to Canvey Island.
123 AD	Christianity comes to Essex.
124 AD	Christianity goes away again (for a short holiday).
1050	The infamous Duke of Ongar proclaims himself King of Essex.
1051	The King of Essex proclaims himself Duke of Ongar.
1052	Reign stops play.
1053	The Duke of Ongar kills the King of Essex during a duel with sawn-off cross bows. 133 not out.
1077	News of King William's conquests hasn't reached Essex yet due to delays in the post.
1187	Still no news of William who has now been dead for at least 100 years. A letter arrives the following day.
1302	The first strawberry appears in Essex.
1303	The second strawberry appears in Essex. Experts estimate that it will take 300 years to make a pot of jam.
1341	The Black Death in Essex.

1342 Black Death T-shirts, mugs and cuddly toys on sale at Woolworth's.

1759 It is nearly six o'clock in Essex.

1848 Railways in Essex. The first train is late, thus setting a trend.

1939 War declared. Essex fights pitched battle with Suffolk until told that it is the *Germans* they should be fighting.

1945 War ends. Pitched battle with Suffolk resumes.

1964 The Beatles avoid Essex.

1971 Britain is decimalized. Essex misses the point.

1973 Britain joins the Common Market. Essex applies to leave Britain.

1986 'Tall Tales of Essex' first broadcast. Essex applies to leave Britain.

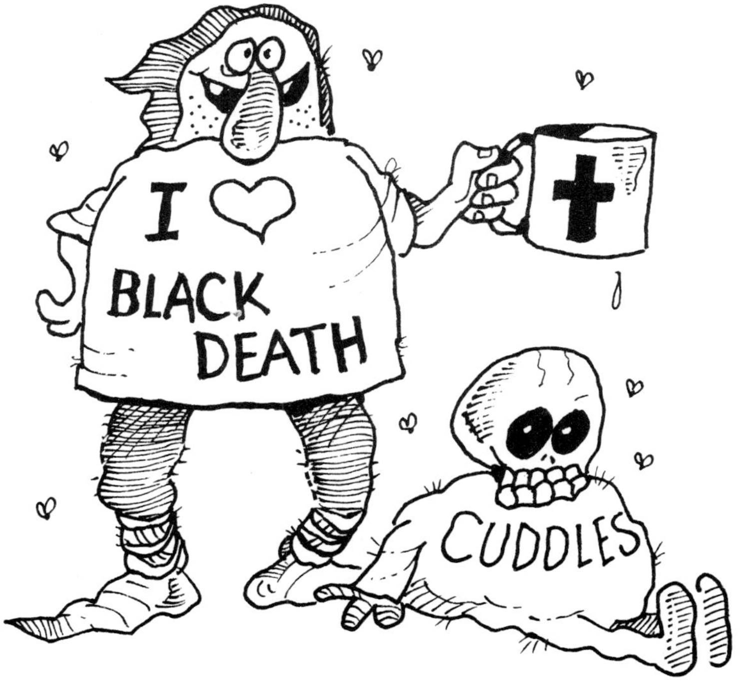

The Aerial Adventures of Moorcock and Bull

I THINK I will be on firm ground when I propose that the *least* natural element to travel about in is the *air*. To mix my metaphors slightly further, I maintain that the human psyche is way out of its depth when suspended seemingly without any logical means of support, miles above solid earth.

I have had the opportunity to travel in several forms of aircraft. These have ranged from the terrifying glider (no engine), the heaving helicopter (no wings), the skittish single-engine (too small) and the gigantic Jumbo Jet (too big).

Of course it is a statistical fact that air travel is as safe as houses (and in the case of the Jumbo Jet as *big* as houses), and yet the worry is still there. Will those wings drop off? Just look at them wobbling about out there! And is the aircraft floor really firmly bolted on? I mean, there's just NOTHING under our feet, is there!

It's not that I have a phobia about flying. It's just that I've never been known to fully relax in the air and let the plane take the strain. Bearing that in mind, I find it incomprehensible that any of us should indulge in flying for the sheer *pleasure* of it. But there they are, poncing about the skies of a weekend in their balloons, hang-gliders, home-made buzz-boxes and reconditioned Spitfires.

The Wright brothers started all this nonsense when they demonstrated the world's first powered flying machine about eighty four years ago in America. Hot on their tails were two brewers from Stansted Mountfitchet, Mr. Stanley Moorcock and Mr. Oliver Bull, who demonstrated what can best be described as the first slightly *under*powered flying machine in Essex.

Moorcock and Bull had followed (when their brewing activities permitted) the exploits of the Wright brothers, with mounting excitement and enthusiasm. However, this excitement rather got the better of Moorcock and Bull, for their first experiment in air travel proved rather embarrassing.

The two brewers owned a field and barn which backed onto their brewery. The field proved ideal as an airfield and the barn, suitable for the necessary construction work and manufacture of their first aircraft. This aircraft, which was based on a design by the French inventor Felix Du Temple (1874) was steam-powered (for those of you who will doubt the veracity of this, I invite you to consult Histories of airflight) and it was ready for it's maiden flight one sunny July morning in 1909.

Moorcock and Bull had, perhaps, slightly rushed things in their understandable desire to get airborne as quickly as possible. With their air machine (called *Flying Pig One)* all stoked up and ready to go, the fearless flitters strapped themselves into the rudimentary cockpit (a couple of wicker chairs), pulled the chocks away and thundered out across the meadow accompanied by a shower of steam, smoke, smutts and confidence.

Later, after they had disentangled themselves from the boundry hedge (and the somewhat buckled aircraft) they set about re-designing the plane so that it would at least get into the air.

Within a short time, Oliver Bull had solved the aerodynamic problem. Closer scrutiny of the plans pinpointed the major fault and without delay, *wings* were added to the airframe. This improved matters no end, and soon our two unflinching fliers were buzzing about the clear blue Essex sky as to the manor born.

Flying Pig One was such a success, that it was soon scrapped and replaced by an upgraded version called *Flying Pig Two.* This machine differed from the first in that it was driven by a petrol engine (raking out the coals at 200 feet was a bit of a bore). This engine created 16 H.P. and drove two pusher propellers mounted at the back of the machine. The wing span was forty feet and the aircraft was launched along a wooden track. A catapult provided the speed to get the whole contraption airborne. *Flying Pig Two* also had a pair of skids built under it which enabled it to land on any ground conditions, however rough. These ground conditions included the Vicar's vegetable patch, the local cricket pavilion, a field full of ripe curly kale, Lord Jeary's tennis court, the village pond, Lord Jeary's bowls green and the main railway line to Kings Lynn.

Needless to say this wanton and distructive display of aeronautic abandon rather upset the local gentry, much used to the peasantry staying in its place, and so a group of the most prominent squires met one evening in order to devise a scheme to put the skids under Moorcock and Bull.

Meanwhile our intrepid twosome, oblivious to the havoc and ill-feeling that they were creating, gaily forged ahead with an even more powerful aircraft. *Flying Pig Three,* was double the horse power and with a new design of airframe, it was able to stay up longer, fly further and be a bit more controllable. This, however, didn't prevent an enraged Lord Jeary from trying to gun the plane down.

This incident occurred during a grouse shoot one Sunday afternoon. What had enraged Lord Jeary, (more indeed than the presence of Moorcock and Bull in their flying machine,) was the way that the grouse had taken refuge aboard the plane as it whizzed past. The canny grouse then hopped off when well clear of the guns. This, indeed was the final straw! Moorcock and Bull just had to be stopped!

The following week, Lord Jeary, aided by the vicar Harry Webb, Sir William Maynes president of the cricket club and an assortment of farmers and residents of Stansted Mountfitchet, proceeded to put into operation their plan to rid themselves, once and for all of that troublesome twosome.

Quantities of white paint, paintbrushes and ladders were obtained and each member of the group was dispatched to a previously identified location. All went smoothly and within hours their tasks were complete. There had been no sign of Moorcock and Bull during that time, and now all that remained was to settle back and await results. If things went according to plan, then very *next* time the two fliers flew off they would never return again. At least not in one piece. And that is precisely what happened. So, just *how* was this achieved? Well, remember,

back in those days, pilots had no instruments or aids to navigation. It was all line of sight, fingers in the wind stuff. Landmarks were the only guide as to where the hell you were at any given moment. It was on *this* understanding that Lord Jeary and his crew worked their trick.

On several flat-roofed buildings dotted around the county painted in big white letters were the words, 'THIS WAY TO STANSTED'. Added to this, in each case, a large white arrow pointed in the exact *opposite* direction to Stansted. Such was the location of each flat-roofed building that any flier who happened upon them would lose all sense of bearing. Moorcock and Bull and already lost all sense of *proportion*, and so their bearings soon went. High up in the sky, that fateful day with their fuel running low, Moorcock and his partner Bull got thoroughly lost and confused as they searched in vain for the elusive Stansted. And it was over Baisingstoke, that our very dizzy duo crashed horribly and fatally. It was no fault of theirs that they chose to land right on top of the Sherborn St. John branch of the Woman's League for Health and Beauty, who were all out on a lawn doing rhythmic callisthenics.

Aviation, of course survived.

Pioneers of powered flight are honoured all over the world. Moorcock and Bull, on the other hand have been totally forgotten. Perhaps it might be a nice idea to erect some sort of memorial to them at the expanding Stansted Airport. After all, it *is* the birth-place of British aviation. On second thoughts, I don't think that the residents of Stansted would appreciate *another* reminder of air travel.

I hear tell that the local gentry are a bit browned off with the idea of a third London Airport on their doorsteps. Indeed, some of them have resorted to an old idea to combat it. If you happen to travel to Stansted today, don't be *too* surprised if you get hopelessly confused and lost. Just take my tip and beware of signposts, painted in big white letters that read, THIS WAY TO STANSTED.

Tall Limericks of Essex

If you have the where-with-all
go to Hatfield Peverel.
But don't be defeated
if you're swindled and cheated
for the people there
have bugger-all!

Gregory Vinter's Vocation

BEFORE we arrive at the point of no return and describe just exactly *what* Gregory Vinter's vocation is, let me put things into some sort of context. That context is, in a word, *Dialects.*

Generally speaking, Essex dialects fall into two categories; The *spoken* and the *written about.* The former is, perhaps slightly less tedious than the latter in my opinion, (an opinion which some people feel should be immediately buried under ten feet of mucklegrum and sprayed with liberal amounts of fuzzle! (Mucklegrum and fuzzle are, of course old Romford dialect words for icecream and lemonade.)

The county of Essex has several dialect appreciation groups, the most active of which is the Bicknacre based Dialect and Liberation of Essex Crafts Society, (or DALECS for short.) This society is currently pressing the Essex Education Authority to introduce compulsory dialect lessons in all the schools in the county. Apparently, this is being given serious consideration as a replacement for the more traditional forms of punishment.

The DALECS have also suggested that it might not be a bad idea if Essex road signs were written in dialect. They argued that it would be quite a nice tourist attraction and would give the region a feeling of identity. As most of the road signs in Essex seem to be written in some sort of dialect already, there doesn't seem to be much mileage in *that* idea.

Another scheme from our friends the DALECS, has been broached to the Independent Broadcasting Authority. DALECS want to be allocated air-time on the new Super Channel. This would mean that Europe would be treated to it's very own Direct Dialect Satellite Television station.

Fortunately, the IBA turned down this idea, which pleased some politicians who feared that Europe (and especially the

Soviet Bloc) might retaliate with Albanian television programmes about knitting in Outer Mongolia or extracts from Stalin's cookery book.

But to return to Essex. Of all the dialects, the really *most* obscure (and that's saying something I can tell you!) comes from a place called Canewdon. The greatest exponent of this dialect, (called 'Canney') is local builder Gregory Vinter. He bills himself, (when he performs at local functions) as a 'Dialect Stand-Up Comedian'. Invariably his audience stands up and walks out but this has not deterred Vinter from spending the last forty years in collecting dire dialect monologues.

Recently, Gregory Vinter published a selection of these monologues under the title, 'Fund Or Looy', which loosely translated means, 'How To Bore The Balls Off A Bull', which in turn is an old agricultural joke meaning 'Fund Or Looy'.

As an example, one of these monologues begins like this.

"Nok, nok. Who's zeer?"

"Tiz oye?"

"Whooze oye?"

"Tiz me!"

"Whooze me?"

"Tiz yur brether!"

"Brether who?"

"Brether me pons fur a nockle!"

Another monologue begins thus:

"Oye met ol Rolly un oye say, 'How be thy un whaat *jub* yer get?' He says, 'Oye be huh *Posstmin,* wich ees butter then *warkin* ther *stretts.*'

I admit that this looks a bit flat on the page, but I'm assured that it's the way he tells 'em. Bearing all that in mind, I shall remember to *avoid* old Rolly when he's out delivering the mail down Canewdon way. The chances are that he might bore something off me!

A few months ago Gregory Vinter took part in the annual World Dialect Championship Series. This was held in Stockholm before an international audience (extracts of which were transmitted by Channel Four at a late hour.) Although Vinter wasn't placed amongst the winners (the top prize went to a Polish gentleman who delivered a lengthy Finnish dialect poem all about greater understanding between mankind, read in the original Finnish) he did receive a special mention from the judges. Just what that special mention *was* is still being translated by a team of cryptographers and language experts at the University of Essex.

As a direct result of his slight success at the Championships, Gregory Vinter has since been presented with an award by Southend Council. He has been given the freedom of the city. Just *which* city, hasn't yet been decided, although Dundee or

Inverness have been mooted.

Recently, Vinter was contacted by a Braintree record producer and he is now engaged in transcribing some of his monologues onto a long playing record. This L.P., with the provisional title of 'Singalong with Fund Or Looy At 33⅓' is due to be released at Christmas time. Vinter hopes that his record will reach a wide public, and it will probably go some way to solve that nagging little problem of what gifts to buy the relatives. The *best* that can be hoped for under these circumstances is that Grandma is stone deaf, and that Uncle Horace can conveniently arrange to drop dead on December the 24th.

And as for the dialects of Essex? Well, as Shakespeare so aptly put it in *King Henry VI part two,* "Have done, for more I hardly can endure."

Edward's Potato Machine

WHAT can't be touched, seen or manufactured? Sounds like another dire question from Trivial Pursuits. In fact, next to banking and insurance, one of the most lucrative services that this country offers to the world is *tourism.* This particular industry is classed, at the end of each fiscal month, as an *invisible earning.* This is, of course not to be confused with 'invisible mending', which is something that we have to do when the trippers depart.

A recent example of regional tourism, (a promotional scheme devised by the worthy burgers of Colchester) involved advertising widely in the Middle East, the sultry pleasures of that fair city. Colchester might not sound like the most obvious playground for a jaded Arab oil millionaire. Not many casinos, racecourses, marinas, mosques, that sort of thing.

In fact, the reasoning went like this. If say, six hundred bountiful shieks came over and spent, for example, £2,000 each then the Corporation coffers would be better off by at least twelve million quid. Conversely, the same ingenious calculation would hold true if, say, *twelve million* Arabs popped over and spent *one* pound each.

In fact, tourism in Essex is a well-established industry. For example, during 1940, quite a few Germans dropped in for the day in their superb Bavarian flying machines. Admittedly they were slightly unwelcome at the time, roaring all over the skies in a typically arrogant manner and littering the countryside with empty cans of sauerkraut and rather loud and deadly high explosives.

The ancient Romans too, spent many a merry away-day in Essex, enriching the culture by having lots of baths, building roads, planning towns and introducing taxation. Some might say that we've never fully recovered from all that.

Our good friends, the Americans continue to invade these shores, cruising over the Atlantic and bringing with them their welcome bonhomie, cash and other sorts of Cruises of a slightly more volatile and directional nature. If nothing else, the Yanks have contributed enormously to the establishment of tourism in Essex, plus the usual protest and feminist movements.

Some might say that we will never fully recover from all that.

One of the earliest examples of tourism was featured in that best seller of 1085AD, *The Brentwood and Hutton Domesday Book*. Chapter 155 mentions a local market gardener called Edward Woolsik. It would seem that in order to raise some much needed venture capital, Edward decided to open his small-holding to tourists. He charged three groats admission, with a cream tea and a ride on the pig thrown in.

People came from far and wide, (one person even came from Harold Wood) and the open-day proved a great success for Edward. He made quite a considerable amount of cash, enough to plough back into the business as well as the lettuce beds.

But news of Edward Woolsik's good fortune had reached other, less charitable ears. So when Edward opened his garden to the public on the following Sunday, three enormous gentlemen confronted him. They were posing as tourists but they, in fact worked for the Duke of Ongar in his recently established Tax Collecting and Customs-Excising Department.

They explained to Edward that in return for a small consideration (paid weekly) they would prevent a herd of *buffalo* from trampling all over his cabbage patch. They also added, for good measure, that they had a swarm of *locusts* straining at the leash plus a thousand or so *thrips* who were a bit on the hungry side. It sounded like an offer that Edward could not reasonably refuse.

But Edward Woolsik was made of sterner stuff. The Duke of Ongar's Ogres didn't frighten *him* (although he was a little worried at the thrip threat.) But this just won't do, he thought. He had worked hard at his business and he didn't intend to fork out his disposable income just to featherbed some parochial potentate. In any case, he concluded, bribes could not be counted as a tax-deductable expense, and in *this* case the tax deductable expense *was* the bribe!

Edward needed time to think. The towering Tax Men seemed in no mood for prevarication. A snap decision was needed. So Edward agreed to their demands. But first, suggested Edward, why not have a trip around the gardens while my wife collects the money? In fact, this was a *ruse,* for Edward had decided on the method by which he could rid himself of the troublesome Tax Men once and for all.

After he had shown the three men examples of his farming techniques, he led them slowly and innocently towards a daub and wattle hut. Within this hut lay a large container half full of peeled potatoes. Assorted bits of machinery were attached to this container. It looked very mysterious. In fact the entire apparatus was a primitive but hightly effective machine that sliced up the potatoes for the lucrative French Fry market in nearby Shenfield.

Edward invited the Duke's men to inspect the spuds for quality. He explained that this could be more easily done if all *three* of them climbed *into* the container. Now, by nature tax men aren't suspicious creatures, and so lulled by a very real sense of false security, the three men climbed in. As soon as they had done this, Edward slammed the heavy lid shut and with an evil and truimphant cackle, started up the slicing machine. Edward then sat on top of the machine to add weight to his measure.

A short while later, Edward's wife returned, carrying a bag of money. Not unnaturally she enquired as to why the spud-slicer was *screaming* like that.

"Oh, don't ye worry yore head about that, my dear," Edward replied smugly. "It's only chipping Ongar Tax Men."

STUDY these two pictures of Old Essex and see if you can spot at least *ten* differences.

The solution is on page 78.

Reg of Epping

ONE of my very favourite films is the 1938 Hollywood production, 'The Adventures Of Robin Hood'. This motion picture, directed by Michael Curtiz and William Keighley, is a superb recreation of Merry Olde England as it never was. The action, photographed on the Warner Bros Burbank backlot (in the original three-strip Technicolor process) has little to equal it even today. What a romantic place History could have been if it had had the likes of Errol Flynn leaping about all over the place. And limpid-eyed Olivia de Havilland as Maid Marion accompanied by the stirring strings of Erich Wolfgang Korngold. I suppose that in reality, Marion was a pock-marked shrew, and Robin, a mead-soaked, toothless sadist, with a neat line in larceny. Still, whatever the *real* truth, Robin Hood certainly put Sherwood Forest into the history books.

Epping Forest, on the other hand, has a slightly lesser claim to fame in the shape of Reginald Hood. Not exactly the stuff that myths are made of, Reg put his mark on the world in the Winter of 1937, and the world went on, regardless.

Reginald Hood was a middle-aged, balding bachelor, invoice clerk for the Gas Light and Coke Company, and probably the *least* successful outlaw ever to live.

Cast your minds back to the Great Epping Mail Van Robbery of 1937, when a large quantity of surplus penny stamps was stolen, just north of Mott Street. It was a daring raid, enacted in broad daylight and the police estimated that the value of the stolen stamps was anything up to nine hundred pounds. It was obviously the work of a master criminal.

Well, Reginald Hood had absolutely nothing to do with all *that.* In fact, at the time of the raid he had been at the Walthamstow Roxy watching Douglas Fairbanks in 'Robin Hood' (1922 version).

Although the mail van robbery filled the papers for a week or so, it was soon overtaken by other events (the latest dance craze, the latest hit crooner; that sort of important thing) and the police were no nearer to catching the culprits.

When Reginald Hood found a few stamps in the road (just *east* of Mott Street) he, unfortunately didn't make the vital connection with the robbery. The stamps he had found were part of the stolen consignment and were easily identified as such because of the manifest fault that they displayed. Close inspection would have revealed that the King's head had been printed back to front. Reg was all unaware of this and just put the stamps in his wallet for later use.

The later use that Reg put one of the stamps to was on a letter he had written to the Chief Constable, complaining about the deplorable crime wave in Essex. Reg used another on a missive to a friend of his in Acrington. The Acrington buddy had an interest in philately and soon spotted the imperfection. He wrote back at once to enquire as to whether Reg had any more of these valuable items. He added, as an afterthought, that the stamp looked just like the ones stolen in the Mott Street raid!

It was then that Reg put two and three together and remembered that he had put one of those stamps on his letter to the Chief Constable! It was at that point that Reg became frantic with worry and apprehension. What should he do? Should he own up to finding the stamps in the road? Would this in turn lead the police to suspect *him* of masterminding the mail van robbery? Poor old Reg got all in a dither at the appauling prospects ahead of him.

As luck would have it, that very evening, as Reg was about to go to bed, there came a loud and insistant knock at his front door. Reg, who lived in a ground-floor maisonnette in Warren Hill, peered fretfully through his net curtains and perceived two large, identically dressed gentlemen waiting outside. One of them appeared to be holding a sheet of paper.

The police, with a warrant! Here they were at last, Reg thought in panic. The midnight knock! The old third degree!

They've come to drag me kicking and screaming down to the police station to give me a good licking!

Without a second's hesitation, Reg scuttled out the back door, leaped over the back fence, and clad only in his pyjamas and dressing gown, escaped to live wild in Epping Forest until the heat died down. As it was Winter time, things got pretty chilly from then on.

The two large, identically dressed gentlemen, were quite unconscious of the train of events that they had set into motion. They were not, as Reg assumed, police officers, but in fact a couple of Jehovah's Witnesses doing a late-night stint. After a bit of the usual hanging about, the leader of the duo stuffed the sheet of paper he was holding through Reg's letter box. Written on it in portentous and prophetic script were the words, "Repent, for catastrophe is at hand!" Unfortunately for Reg, those words were of little comfort.

In his flight from certain arrest, Reg remembered an old tree-house deep in the forest which he used to play in when a child. The tree-house still existed and Reg found it, without much difficulty, still intact. He had also stumbled upon a discarded Fortnam and Mason hamper (even then Epping was a prosperous area), but soon his rich diet of Cornish Crab Bisque, Brandy Butter, Cranberry Sauce, Patum Peperium and Quail's Eggs in Brine soon ran out and Reg, in desperation, turned to stealing.

He tried his hand at highway robbery, but had to hastily abandon the idea when he was nearly run over and killed by a fast City Coach which steadfastly ignored him when he leapt out in front of it waving an imitation gun made of twigs. Reg then resorted to mugging. But as the term hadn't been invented back in 1937, Reg had to use a broken tea-cup. This, he threw at a tramp who was shuffling by. The tramp responded by picking up the tea-cup and chucking it back at Reg. It caught him a glancing blow on the lip, thus reducing his confidence to an even lower ebb.

Food and drink became a priority for Reg. Close to delirium due to the deleterious effects of cold and hunger, Reg spotted a charabanc parked in a layby. The charabanc, full of Spurs supporters on the way home, had pulled up for refreshments. Crates of brown ale were being unloaded from the back. Reg crept closer and hid in the ditch beside the layby, waiting his chance to grab a bottle or two of the life-giving liquid. Several of the Spurs supporters had taken advantage of this stopover and proceeded to unload *another* form of liquid. In the gloom, they totally failed to notice Reg crouching in the ditch, although their combined aim was faultless. Reg was a bit pissed off at that point, as well as being rather wet and smelly!

Reg squelched back to his tree-house hide-out, cursing the day that he had ever found those wretched stamps in the road! To cap it all, he found that the tree-house had been requisitioned by the same tramp he had thrown the cup at.

And so Reg, the would-be Robin Hood of Epping Forest reached the end of his short and pointless road. Suffering from extreme hypothermia, Reg staggered about the forest, bumping into Willow, Larch and Elm without prejudice. Finally, he came upon an empty car, parked off the road. The car's doors were unlocked, and Reg, totally exhausted, climbed in. What Reg had failed to notice in his delirium was that the parked car was a black Wolseley. A black Wolseley with a *bell* on the bumper and a sign which read POLICE.

When the absent police officers eventually returned (they had, if fact been out looking for car thieves), they found Reg curled up on the back seat, utterly dead from exposure.

Because Reg was dressed in night attire, the police had some difficulty in identifying him. they assumed, at the outset, that he had sleep-walked his way around the forest or that he was some kind of nocturnal sex fiend with a penchant for starvation. Eventually, after his photograph had been published in the 'Epping Enquirer', he was recognised by a neighbour who thought Reg was a bit potty anyway.

Later, when the police, on behalf of the coroner, tried to contact Reg's only living relative, (an aged aunt who lived in a particularly inaccessible part of Australia), the letter that they had sent was returned unopened. This was due, ironically, to incorrect postage.

No.1 The Slowest Man In Essex

THIS photograph taken at Liverpool Street railway station in 1962, shows Michael Robbins (back to camera) who claims to be the slowest man in the whole of Essex. Evidence of this can be found by visiting Liverpool Street station today. There you will see Michael Robbins *still* waiting for his train.

All Steamed Up

FOR those of us dedicated, or for that matter opulent enough to contemplate travelling by rail these days, it will not have gone unnoticed that the rail services in the county of Essex have undergone something of a transformation in recent months.

New buildings, refurbished rolling stock, natty red-coloured platform seats full of cunningly arranged drainage holes that are guaranteed to leave a lasting impression on the unwary traveller (particularly if the wind blows in a certain direction). All this, of course, is only part of the Grand Plan designed with some care by Network SouthEast to improve the services beyond the dreams of Alresford. It is to be hoped that this British Rail Utopia of soft lights, deep-pile carpets, trains that very nearly run on time and enquiry-desk telephones that almost get answered, will be with us very soon.

One railway station to benefit from all this wonderful vicissitude is Chelmsford. Situated half way down Duke Street (or half way up, depending upon which direction you approach it), this once crumbling Victorian pile is now being skillfully transformed (or *has* been skillfully transformed, depending upon whether you purchased this book at the time of publication or picked it up at a jumble sale in Bolton) into something closely resembling a rural shopping arcade.

The railway connection with Chelmsford goes back many years and no history of rail transportation would be complete without mention of Neville Brunswick.

Neville Basil Brunswick, to give him his full name, was a nineteenth century inventor, fanatic and man of independent means. He can also lay claim to being one of the Counties truely forgotten pioneers. At least forgotten until today, for I have discovered that it was Neville Brunswick who, in 1823 demonstrated the first steam locomotive ever seen in Essex.

The South had Trevithick. The North had Stephenson, but *Essex* had Brunswick, and his first locomotive, which was called the *Puffing Willy*, made its debut one fine Autumn day to much applause from the crowd that had gathered to watch.

This embryonic engine, built by Brunswick at a cost of £17/6/3d (quite a lot for those days) was of the centre-flue boiler type with four-coupled drive. It ran on a short circular track to a gauge of five foot one inch and was fired with special soft coal imported from the Russian mining town of Vaarg. Records have shown that the circular track was laid out on land that eventually became the forecourt of Chelmsford railway station.

Unfortunately, during the very first demonstration when the Puffing Willy set off on its maiden circuit, the hard-pressed boiler totally exploded, showering the happy crowd of onlookers with bits of metal, hot steam and rather hard, soft coal.

The fault proved to be some poorly made leather boiler rivets, (a not uncommon problem at the time) and although nobody was killed, several pregnant sheep in an adjoining field quite spontaneously aborted on the spot.

But Brunswick had proved that his engine worked (apart from the rivets that is) and the Puffing Willy achieved a top speed, (incredible for the age) of six miles an hour.

This prompted several learned gentlemen to speculate on the dire effects that might be wrought on the human frame at such a reckless velocity. The final word on the subject was left to the Bishop of Chelmsford who remarked that, "If the Good Lord had meant us to go round in circles at six miles an hour, he would have given us one leg shorter than the other!"

Fired with the undoubted success of his engine, Neville Brunswick then built the world's first underground railway, utilizing the abandoned quarry tunnels at Little Waltham. These vast, arched caverns (now closed to the public) that stretched for miles under the Walthams (Great and Little) were once mined for the famous Broomfield Borax, but were closed down when the world borax price collapsed due to overproduction in Hong Kong.

SEE THE
PUFFING
WILLY
HERE
TODAY

Such was the layout of the tunnels, that Brunswick encountered little expense with the construction work, save for a bit of track-laying, a rather primitive signalling system, a few oil lamps and copious quantities of Greene King to slake the thirsts of the borax-coated construction crew.

When complete, the railway ran for at least 2000 yards. The engine that was used was an upgraded version of the Puffing Willy, (the rivets problem having been sorted out) and it was named with faultless logic, the *Puffing Mole.*

Neville Brunswick was now ready to go and he advertised his new venture to the public at 6d a ride. People flocked to this new wonder of the modern age and on the opening day all the coaches were packed to bursting point when the first trip set off.

The unforeseen problem that occured was that all the smoke and fumes from the Puffing Mole soon polluted the tunnels to such an extent that the journey ended with one hundred and fifty fare-paying corpses enjoying the inaugural run.

At the official inquiry, held a few weeks later at the Shire Hall in Chelmsford, Neville Brunswick was absolved from all blame. His defence rested on the fact that he didn't know that smoke could damage your health. As a gesture to the relatives of the deceased, Brunswick refunded the full cost of the underground ride plus a free ticket on whatever his next project turned out to be.

What Brunswick's *next* project turned out to be was a unique *mono-rail* system to run on elevated tracks. His plan was to link the hamlets of Chignall Smealy and Shellow Bowells and provide the inhabitants of these villages with a pleasant aerial journey. A new and improved steam locomotive was constructed and christened with the wholly apt, (if mouth-mangling name) of the *Puffing Puffin.*

But trouble was looming. It seems that the elevated tracks, which traversed perfectly flat farm land, had been built *too* high up. The reason for this was due to some confusion in reading the plans. Brunswick had commissioned a local scaffolding company, (Richard Turpin and Co: "We stick 'em up.") and their

Brunswick's Monorail (with bird scarer)

works foreman, who just happened to be dyslexic had transposed inches and feet into *feet* and *yards.* The upshot of all this was that when the first train set off on a test run along the towering trackway, it immediately ran into a bank of low cloud and the driver was tragically killed when a migrating and surprised flock of Tawny Pipits invaded his cab.

But by this time people were getting a little fed up with Neville Brunswick, and in any case the Eastern Counties Railway Company had at last opened a line to London. So the writing was well and truely on the time-table for poor old Neville.

By 1845, he had declined to such an extent that nobody was prepared to listen to his most ambitious scheme. And so the world was robbed of his 'Heavier Than Air Locomotive'. The *Puffing Albatross* never took off. Indeed, it proved to be just *too* far ahead of its time. A recent study of the plans has revealed that the engine would have needed a runway 350 miles long in order for it to achieve a take-off speed of 175 mph.

By 1850, rail travel in Essex was well established with lines to places as far apart as Thorpe Bay and Wendens Ambo. Neville Brunswick just couldn't compete nor indeed justify his little local schemes. He was declared bankrupt in 1851 and at that point just ran out of steam.

He ended his days, a sad, forgotten and lonely pioneer in the best British tradition. He died at the early age of 56 in a paupers bed at Chelmsford and Essex Hospital, hollow eyed, grey of hair and dribbling.

As one fellow patient remarked of him at the time, "Ah yes, Neville Brunswick, I remember him. Y'know, he always struck me as a little loco."

No.2 The Tallest Tree In Essex

THE tallest tree in Essex (The Siberian Larch) once stood at the junction of Gubbins Lane and Squirrels Heath Road in Harold Wood. Standing well over 100 feet tall, the tree fell down in a gale in 1960. This surprised the driver of the Austin Cambridge who was doing a perfect right hand turn into oblivion at the time.

No. 3 The Driest Place In Essex

THE driest place in Essex is Great Wakering. The wettest place in Essex isn't Hastings (where the picture was taken).

Our happy trio of holiday makers are wishing (judging from their expressions) that they were in the driest place in Essex.

About Anglia

ESSEX has a plethora of radio stations, but rather a dearth of television stations. In fact, *none* at all. However this is not strictly true, for *Anglia Television* has a studio in Chelmsford, (New London Road) from where it transmits the occasional 'news' story.

Anglia Television has its headquarters in Norwich (near Market Avenue) and although this book is ostensibly about Essex, I would like to make a brief diversion at this point and trundle off into the wilds of Norfolk and present a short history of this much respected and world famous company.

Anglia Television officially began transmitting from its studios (a converted Corn Exchange) on October 27th 1959. Test transmissions had actually started two months earlier when engineers broadcast a film of a Norfolk turkey laying an egg. The inaugural programmes had similar entertainment value and got the station off to a flying start. The Norfolk turkey film has since been preserved and is still frequently used at training sessions for aspirant television producers.

The Anglia Knight

The knight is used as the channel identification for the station, although it would appear not to have any historical connection with the region. The knight (modelled on the statue of Richard Coeur de Lion, which stands outside the Houses of Parliament) is over 100 years old and is made of sterling silver to the weight of 700 ounces. It was commissioned originally by the King of the Netherlands as a prize for horse races, falconry and other sports. In 1850 it was won by an Englishman and remained in the possession of the victor's family until 1959.

The model was adapted slightly for use by Anglia Television

with the addition of a pennon on the lance. This model is laboriously hand-cranked on a turn-table by trainee television directors at the start of some programmes.

The music that is heard when the knight is on the air is part of Handel's 'Water Music' arranged by Sir Malcolm Sargent. Water, as a motif probably refers to the Norfolk Broads. However, it is a well-known fact that water as a substance is completely unknown in the hospitality rooms of Anglia Television, as this writer can attest.

News and Current Affairs.

The popular 'About Anglia' magazine and news programme was first broadcast in 1960. Since then the show has gone from strength to strength and it now reaches an audience of anything up to three million every weekday evening. As a guide to the region and its news, it is an invaluable programme, but much of the show's appeal stems from its Presenters. Particular mention must be made of anchor-man Graham Bell. His urbane and gently ironic style has brought him many fans over the countless years that he has been with the show. Graham might be startled to learn that he has a fan club in Russia. During the summer months, due to atmospheric quirks, the show is picked up in the pretty east-coast town of Vaarg. Evidence of Graham's fame can be heard from Vaargites as they imitate his well-known catch-phrase, "It's a bootiful day, boy!"

Drama.

In 1978, the writer of short stories, Ronald Dahl suggested to the drama department an idea for a series of plays that would have international appeal. The Head of Production liked the idea and a series was commissioned under the provisional title of 'Tales of the Unexpurgated'. This was quickly changed to 'Tales of the Predictable'. A further and final change was ordered by the Head of Production, who after seeing a few of the completed programmes at a preview, rather inexplicably chose the now familiar title, 'Tales of the Unexpected'.

Something which is still rather obscure is the exact reason for the change in Ronald Dahl's christian name. Exhaustive research has shown that the reason was probably due to a typing error at the final contract stage. In any event the 'N' got left out, hence the distinctive 'Roald', a name that the author has laboured under with fantastic and much deserved success ever since.

Survival Anglia Ltd.

The Survival Unit produces superb nature films which are purchased for showing at home and abroad. From its earliest days, (turkeys and eggs etc) the Unit has presented us with many aspects of the natural world. The most famous programme, made in conjunction with Oxford Scientific Films was the incredible 'Secret World of the Mole'. Photographed with special lenses that could see in the dark, nothing was hidden from the probing eye of the camera. In fact, this wonderful film almost missed its transmission date. The local office of the Special Branch had got wind of it and raided the production offices. The programme (and off-cuts) were hurriedly confiscated and examined for leaks. Fortunately the programme was returned intact in time for showing.

Live From Norwich
Finally, a brief mention of one of the most popular programmes ever produced by Anglia Television. 'Sale Of The Century' was conceived as a bingo version of 'Mastermind' and 'University Challenge'. The programme, hosted by genial and much lampooned Nicholas Parsons, revolved around three contestants who, after answering terribly hard questions like who is Prince Phillip married to or, what is the capital of Chad, got the chance to bid for valuable prizes. These usually ranged from holidays for two in Eastbourne or a years subscription to the *Essex Countryside.* The show had popular appeal and was rarely out of the top ten ratings for the length of its run.

It is interesting to note that by producing this programme from the very heart of Norwich, Anglia Television was (and is) continuing the historic traditions associated with the old Corn Exchange building. Long may it do so.

The Ghastly Ghost of Sandon

DRIVERS amongst us cannot fail but be aware that Essex has, at last been dragged kicking and screaming into the motoring age. Bypasses are springing up all over the place (which as a metaphor leaves a little to be desired as well as boggling the mind.) Such is the proliferation of private transport that one member of the County Council was heard to confess that, "the horseless carriage is here to stay!" Motorists now rejoice at the prospect of being able to travel the breadth of London via the marvellous M25 during the rush hour (and I use the verb 'rush' advisedly) in almost as much time as it used to take.

Naturally, not everybody is so ecstatic about the arrival of motorways and bypasses, especially if they have a habit of cutting straight across the backs of gardens, creating unacceptable amounts of noise and fumes and rattling the budgie off its perch.

Which brings us to a day in 1933 when, at a meeting of the *CHELMSFORD HIGHWAYS, FOOTPATHS and WHERE TO POSITION TRAFFIC LIGHTS IN THE MOST INCONVENIENT PLACE COMMITTEE,* it was decided to construct a new road linking the A414 with the notorious traffic blackspot of Howe Green. It was agreed that construction should begin as soon as possible and the plans were hastily drawn up to beat the dead-line; (ie. the Chairman going on holiday.) The fact that this new highway was to run slap bang across the land of a Sandon potato farmer called Barnaby Booth, hardly counted as a consideration. Back in those days, little things like public consultations were unknown, or at least brushed aside, and so the *first* thing that Barnaby Booth knew of the new road was when a van load of construction workers arrived early one Monday morning and had dug up three acres of best King Edwards be-

SANDON SAND

fore one could say, 'Planning Blight'.

Understandably, Barnaby Booth was a little upset at this wanton act of municipal vandalism. His livelihood was being ripped up before his eyes without a good morning or by-your-leave! A phone call to the council offices did little to clarify matters. He was brusquely informed that all the necessary paperwork had been completed and the compulsory purchase order had been sent out. Booth argued that he had received nothing in the way of notification and demanded that work stop immediately! This prompted the council official to quote the famous 'glacier' dictum. (For those of you who are unfamiliar with this dictum it is this: It is easier to stop a glacier that it is to stop Chelmsford Council.) End of dictum.

Incidentally, it later transpired that Booth's compulsory purchase order had, due to a hiccup in the typing pool, been misaddressed, not to Sandon but to *Sandringham.* This caused a flutter in royal circles and an immediate loss of an O.B.E. to the committee chairman.

In the face of all this perfidious perturbation, Barnaby Booth could do little but stand and watch as the road was driven through his acres and completed in record time.

The pristine road, as straight as a die, had neatly bisected his farm, and as there was no crossing, he had to drag his tractor half way round Chelmsford in order to reach the other side of his land. It was on one such frustrating trip that Booth conceived a scheme (by way of retribution) to get his own back on the wicked old council.

On the night before the day of the Grand Opening Ceremony, with a full moon illuminating the scene, Barnaby Booth began a fearsome construction. He worked like a demon, possessed it seemed with some internal and infernal fire until at last his mighty work was complete.

What Barnaby Booth had been doing was simply to build a brick wall right across the new road. This wall (built with materials that Booth was going to use on a new storage shed) stood ten feet high and straddled both lanes of the road to a width of fifteen feet.

Satisfied that his wall was complete, Barnaby Booth settled down, totally exhausted behind the wall to await the dawn and the reaction of the council.

Unfortunately, and as luck would have it, Booth's triumph was short-lived. It transpired that the Sandon sand that Booth had mixed with his cement was only of motorway standard, and so as a consequence it soon cracked and crumbled, causing the enormous wall to collapse under its own weight, right on top of the snoozing Booth.

The following morning, the Grand Opening Committee was confronted with an inexplicable heap of bricks and a mashed potato farmer lying underneath.

Later at the inquest, the coroner recorded a verdict of death by misadventure on Barnaby Booth. This, he added, was due in equal parts to Booth's unsound mind at the time and also his unsound wall.

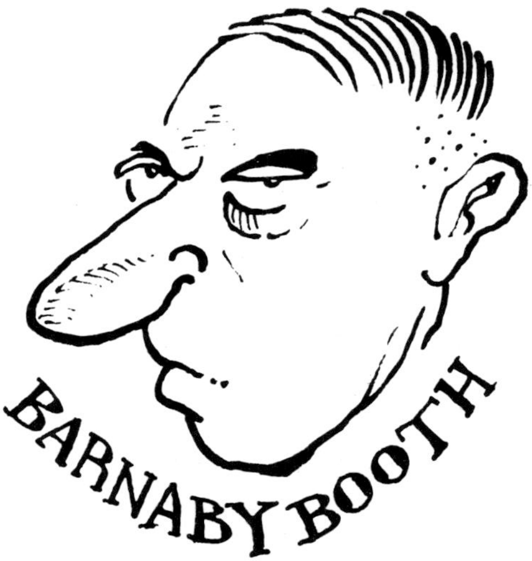

'The Barnaby Booth Barricade', as the local press dubbed it was soon forgotten and the road continued on its way, unmolested until 1985, when the long awaited Chelmsford bypass began construction. Study of aerial maps will show that part of this new bypass was constructed over the *exact* route of the old road that crossed Barnaby Booth's potato farm all those years ago.

Now bearing all that in mind, it may in some way go towards explaining what can only be described as an *apparition* on the bypass.

To put it in context, imagine the Sandon stretch of the bypass, early in the morning as the mists roll in from the pasture lands, creating a monochrome haze, heavy with moisture and foreboding.

It was in just such conditions, a few months ago, that a startled motorist reported the following incident to the police. To use his own words from the report; "There I was, driving along towards my office in Brentwood, when all of a sudden, there up ahead of me, stretched right across the road was this *thing*. And do you know, it looked just like a bloody great ghostly *brick wall!*"

Tall Limericks of Essex

A man who lived in Gants Hill
had trouble paying his
electricity bill.
So he adjusted the meter
and switched on his heater
and fused all the lights
in Mistley.

No. 4 The Essex Man Who Was Adolf Hitler's Double

ALBERT Brown, pictured here at Frinton with his wife in 1959, had for years, the misfortune to look like Adolf Hitler.

His wife Eva said, "Albert was constantly reviled and cursed where ever he went. But things have changed since we had the plastic surgery. Now he's a new person." (Mrs. Brown is on the left of the picture.)

Tall Trivial Quiz of Essex

THIS quiz is designed to test your knowledge of Essex. Answer each question to the best of your ability (no cheating!) and keep a note of your answers: either (A), (B) or (C). At the end of the quiz your *Tall Trivial Rating* can be easily assessed.

Q *Who copied the building techniques that were used on the A127 Southend Arterial Road?*

(A) Adolf Hitler.
(B) Ramasses the Second.
(C) Genghis Khan.

Answer: (A) Pre-war autobahns all led to Southend.

Q *Where in Essex can you walk on water?*

(A) Hanningfield Reservoir.
(B) The River Blackwater.
(C) In the street.

Answer: (C) Most Essex drains get blocked each year.

Q *Where can you find the ugliest building in Essex?*
(A) Chelmsford.
(B) Chelmsford.
(C) Chelmsford.
Answer: (D) Braintree. (You thought that this quiz was going to be as easy as A.B.C. didn't you!)

Q *What does the ugliest building in Essex look like?*
(A) Paycocke's House.
(B) Colchester Castle.
(C) Priors Hall Barn.
Answer: Yes. (or (D) 315 Chignall Way, Chelmsford.)

Q *What is a resident of Pitsea called?*
(A) A twit.
(B) A Pitseat.
(C) A Pixie.
Answer: (A) I am of course referring to Mr Julian Fosdyke-Smythe, stockbroker from No 10 Brickworks Lane, Pitsea.

Q *Who said, 'I'm in charge!'?*
(A) The Manager of British Rail Eastern Region.
(B) Bruce Forsyth.
(C) Charlie Drake.
Answer: (A) Also (B) . . . but then Bruce Forsyth said it as a joke.

Q *Who said, 'You lucky people!'?*
(A) The Manager of British Rail Eastern Region.
(B) Terry Wogan.
(C) Tommy Trinder.
Answer: (A) The Manager was referring to his new time-table. (Also (C) Tommy Trinder. He was joking too.)

Q *Who said, 'Beam me up, Scottie!'?*

(A) The Manager of British Rail Eastern Region.
(B) Patrick Moore.
(C) Rob Roy.

Answer: (A) The Manager of British Rail Eastern Region is alleged to have uttered this when confronted by an irate delegation of 'lucky' commuters.

Q *What is the County Accumulator?*

(A) A battery.
(B) A bug, a pen, a keyring, a badge and a car-sticker.
(C) The rates bill.

Answer: (B) Now come on, admit it. You've never listened to The Mark Thomas show on BBC Essex have you!

Q *What are Maplin Sands?*

(A) Sand.
(B) Wet.
(C) A 'sixties' holiday camp in the North Sea.

Answer: (A) and (B) I'm not going on holiday with *you* if you answered (C)!

Q *Where is Tolleshunt D'Arcy?*

(A) Near Colchester.
(B) Near Romford.
(C) Living in Spain under an assumed name.

Answer: (A) Although last seen boarding the Harwich ferry.

Q *Why is Essex called* Essex?

(A) Because it didn't want to be called Gladys.
(B) Because it is East of Sex.
(C) Because it is an acronym.

Answer: (C) The acronym stands for Eastern Society (of) Superannuated Elderly Xenophobes. Not many people know that.

Scores

Mostly *A*'s. Good show! You know as much about Essex as *I* do (which isn't much).
Mostly *B*'s. Not bad. Try a bit harder next time or I'll set the dogs on you.
Mostly *C*'s. Hopeless! Take a cold shower and report at once to Matron!
Mostly *F*'s. Sorry, you're obviously having a great deal of difficulty in understanding this book, or perhaps you're reading another book altogether. Just try and pay attention next time!

Tall Limericks of Essex

An arsonist both wicked and dire
would try to set people on fire.
He would creep up behind them
and try to alight them
especially at Burnham-on-Crouch

No. 5 The Smallest Fisherman In Essex

BARNEY Williams, who lives in Tollesbury is, by far, the smallest fisherman in Essex. Standing only 24 inches high in his waders, Barney can be seen regularly fishing on the River Blackwater. Our picture shows Barney out in his boat looking for gudgeon.

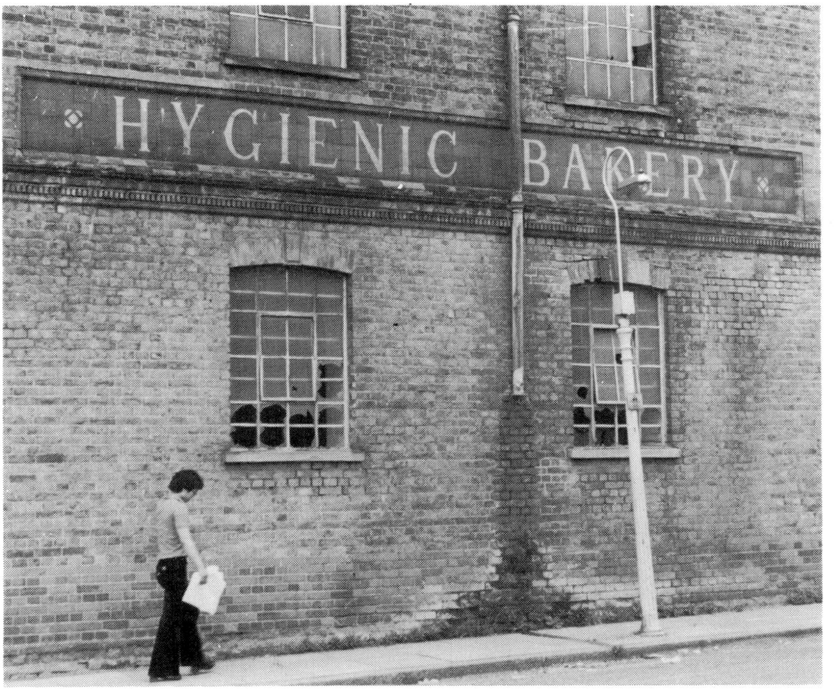

No. 6 The Latest Chinese Take-Away in Essex

'THE Hygienic Billericay Bread Roll Bakery' (which is a devil of a mouthful for a Chinaman) was opened in Billericay town centre last year. Planning permission was granted on the first application (in itself highly unusual) with the proviso that the new building conformed to and blended in with its surroundings. Architect Ling Poo Yung (seen here inspecting the finished building) achieved this with his innovative and award-winning 'Essex Look' design.

Tall Rambles of Essex
No. 1 Bradwell-on-Sea

I'VE prepared for this book, two rambles around well-known areas in Essex. These rambles have never been attempted before and to help you find your way I've illustrated them with some schematic maps. These maps, I should point out, are not to scale. However, if you follow them carefully then I can't be held responsible for the consequences.

The first ramble is in the area known as Bradwell. Unfortunately, Bradwell is perhaps the most boring place to visit in Essex (next to Canvey Island that is). The architecture is tedious and without any charm. The wildlife is unpleasant if not down right dangerous. The views are mind-numbingly barren and the people who live there certainly deserve to do so.

But don't let me try to put you off visiting Bradwell. For all its shortcomings (and they don't come any shorter), the place has a lot to offer the rambler. The sheer muck and filth that one encounters on the walk is something that will stick in the memory for hours. Something that definitely *won't* stick with you is the 'real' ale served up at the 'Three Headed Duck'. It gave me a picturesque case of diarrhoea after the first pint! Also avoid the village church (they charge an *exit* fee). Come to think of it, avoid the village all together.

The high point (at least two feet) of any visit to Bradwell must be the nuclear power station. Constructed at least 25 years ago in a style of architecture known generically as 'International Lavatory', this magnificent pile is a glowing reminder to us all that Great Britain is well in the forefront of nuclear technology.

Like similar plants around the world, it has been carefully designed to last until it goes wrong. This is a great comfort to the people who live in the area (you can recognise them quite easily by the way they *twitch* all the time).

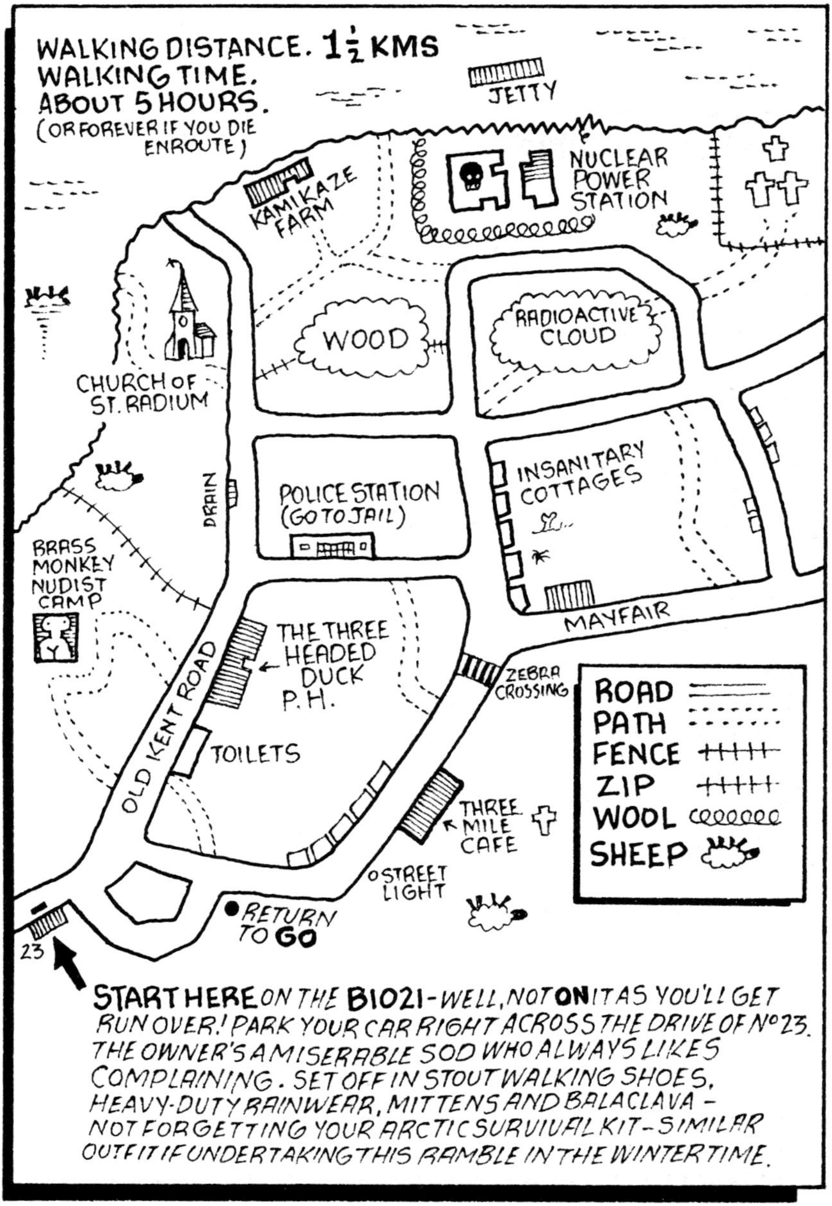
WALKING DISTANCE. 1½ KMS
WALKING TIME.
ABOUT 5 HOURS.
(OR FOREVER IF YOU DIE ENROUTE)
JETTY
KAMIKAZE FARM
NUCLEAR POWER STATION
CHURCH OF ST. RADIUM
WOOD
RADIOACTIVE CLOUD
DRAIN
POLICE STATION (GO TO JAIL)
INSANITARY COTTAGES
BRASS MONKEY NUDIST CAMP
THE THREE HEADED DUCK P.H.
MAYFAIR
ZEBRA CROSSING
OLD KENT ROAD
TOILETS
THREE MILE CAFE
STREET LIGHT
RETURN TO GO
23
ROAD
PATH
FENCE
ZIP
WOOL
SHEEP
START HERE ON THE B1021 - WELL, NOT ON IT AS YOU'LL GET RUN OVER! PARK YOUR CAR RIGHT ACROSS THE DRIVE OF Nº 23. THE OWNER'S A MISERABLE SOD WHO ALWAYS LIKES COMPLAINING. SET OFF IN STOUT WALKING SHOES, HEAVY-DUTY RAINWEAR, MITTENS AND BALACLAVA - NOT FORGETTING YOUR ARCTIC SURVIVAL KIT - SIMILAR OUTFIT IF UNDERTAKING THIS RAMBLE IN THE WINTER TIME.

At the end of your ramble (if you arrive at that point and in one piece) then you may be tempted to try a 'cream tea' at the *Three Mile Cafe.* This is not advised. In any case, I doubt that you will be in a fit state to lift the cup, let alone enjoy its contents. The cream in the tea (at least when *I* tried it) was an interesting shade of green. The rock-cakes and pastry; an odd shade of red. The proprietor of the cafe had a similar hue, tinged with the occasional dash of yellow. In fact, the *Three Mile Cafe* was the only place in Bradwell to have any local colour at all.

Bradwell, then (not forgetting the On-Sea) is certainly worth a visit by the indiscriminate.

Please note the small error that has crept into my map. The 'Brass Monkey' nudist camp doesn't exist. That was just wishful thinking on my part. Sorry.

Tall Rambles of Essex
No. 2 Grays Thurrock

MY second ramble for this book is to Grays Thurrock. Grays Thurrock is a fascinating area which comprises the hamlets of West Thurrock, Little Thurrock, Chadwell St. Mary and North Stifford.

From its northern heights one can perceive the River Thames as it rolls majestically along, past the cement works and on down to the Gravesend waste disposal plant. In fact, such is the clarity of the air at this point that it is possible to see right into Kent, almost as far as Horsmonden, (which is quite far enough, believe me.)

Part of the attraction of walking this area is the way that the rambler will come across the totally unexpected. For example, a multi-car pile up on the M25 at junction 31. This is something that you would certainly miss if you didn't occasionally leave your vehicle and walk around.

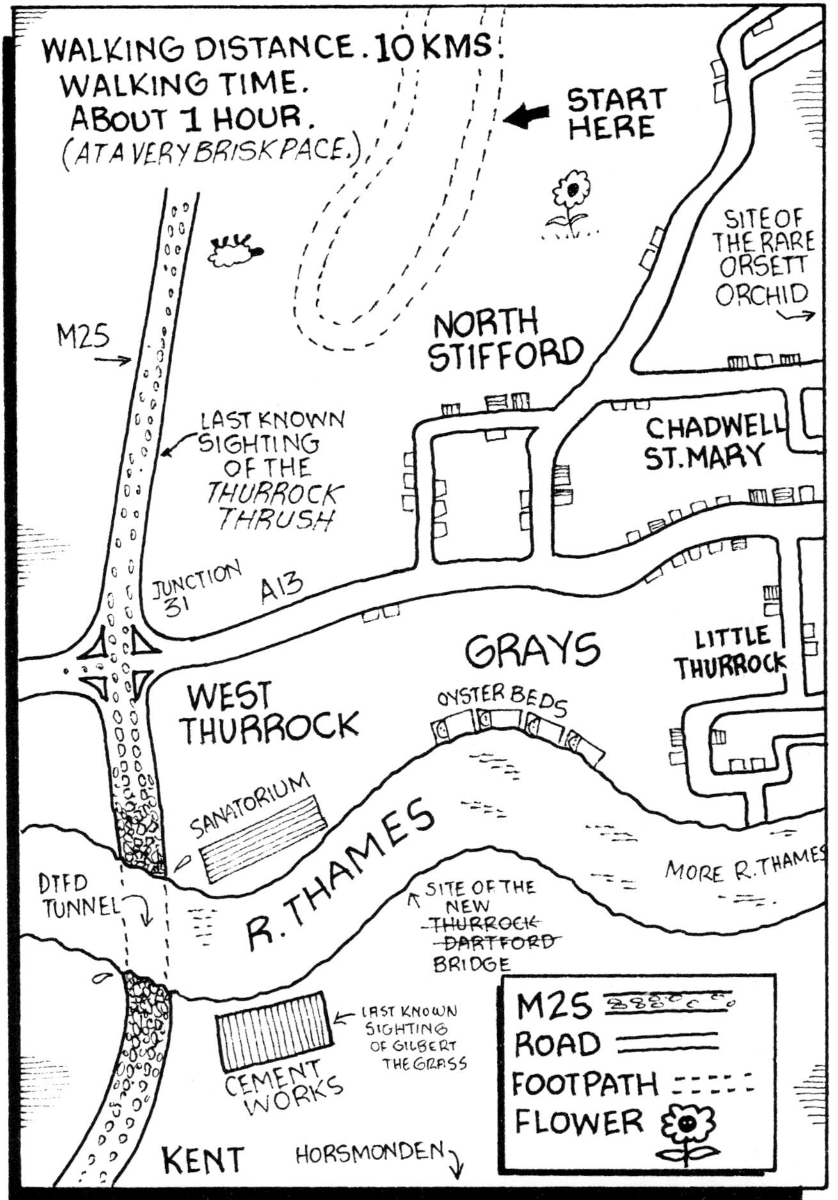
WALKING DISTANCE. 10 KMS.
WALKING TIME.
ABOUT 1 HOUR.
(AT A VERY BRISK PACE.)
START HERE
SITE OF THE RARE ORSETT ORCHID
NORTH STIFFORD
M25
LAST KNOWN SIGHTING OF THE THURROCK THRUSH
CHADWELL ST.MARY
JUNCTION 31
A13
GRAYS
LITTLE THURROCK
WEST THURROCK
OYSTER BEDS
SANATORIUM
R.THAMES
MORE R.THAMES
DTFD TUNNEL
SITE OF THE NEW ~~THURROCK DARTFORD~~ BRIDGE
LAST KNOWN SIGHTING OF GILBERT THE GRASS
CEMENT WORKS
M25
ROAD
FOOTPATH
FLOWER
KENT
HORSMONDEN

But to be serious for one minute, Grays Thurrock is now one of the last remaining spoilt regions in Essex. It is for this reason that I urge you to follow my directions with the utmost care. The last thing we want is careless feet disturbing the flora and fauna. As it is, the poor old Thurrock Thrush is nearly extinct. (This is not to be confused with the Bradwell Bunny, which due to the peculiar ecological conditions in that area *looks* like the Thurrock Thrush.)

Also take note of the variety of native Speedwell growing beside the A13. I counted at least 25 different types before I was unexpectedly run over by a passing push-bike. But these little hazards are a way of life to the really dedicated rambler. Another problem is that of litter. I must confess that I was arrested and fined for dropping litter in Grays Thurrock. It was only a Polo wrapper, but that's not the point. It really *does* pay to follow the country code. In that way, the natural and architectural beauty of a place like Grays Thurrock can be preserved for generations to come. Think of the pride in your voice when you tell your grandchildren that Grays Thurrock is only there because *you* looked after it.

Incidentally, West Thurrock is twinned with the Russian East Coast town of Vaarg, another area of outstanding natural beauty, (once you get past the razor-wire and mine fields that is).

Tall Limericks of Essex

A lady who hailed from South Weald
made love to young men in a field.
She was totally immoral
of that there's no quarrel
but she ruined the wheat at Crays Hill

No. 7 The Most Avant-Garde Film Maker In Essex

AN obscure film director called Julian Platt, who lives in Danbury. His latest epic is called 'No Views Of Essex'. This film runs for five hours and consists of nothing but a blank screen. The photograph reveals how Julian achieves this remarkable effect.

Albert Docker's Commission

WHAT'S got the longest one in the whole world? No, you're wrong, and in any case it would look ridiculous. I'll give you a clue. It stretches out proudly into the Thames estuary for at least a mile. Of course, it's none other than *Southend pier!* However, the main trouble with such a gigantic protuberance is that bits of it keep getting bashed into and knocked off.

It was in 1908 (after the tenth tiresome hit and run in as many months) that Southend Council decided that as things were getting a bit out of hand, it was time to *DO* something. After all, the image of their town as a genteel fun-loving watering place for the great unwashed of Essex was suffering as a consequence. All this nautical vandalism just had to stop! I mean, who would want to spend a happy holiday in a town with no pier? (Or at least with an expurgated version of one.)

So the Council voted to commission an architect to completely re-design the pier and make it boat-bash proof.

The job was put out to tender and as an added incentive, a prize was offered for the best design. In fact, as the prize wasn't particularly tempting (a free ticket to ride on the pier railway) the designs fell rather short of expectations. To be honest, no designs were submitted at all, (at least by any reputable firm,) and so the commission fell, eventually, to a little-known architect called Albert Docker.

Actually, Albert Docker *was* known to the Chairman of the tendering committee, who happened to be Mr. *Joseph* Docker, father of the afore mentioned Albert. This fact in no way swayed the judgement of the tendering committee. A committee member, Mr. *Fred* Docker correctly pointed out that his nephew had quite a bit of experience as an architect. Mrs. *Sylvia* Docker (committee member) pointed to her son's past successes and

GOOD YEAR

cited his tasteful design for telegraph poles on Canvey Island. Mr. *Roger* Docker (committee member) also mentioned his brother's imaginative plan for a speculative housing project on Maplin Sands. *Lucy* and *Martin* Docker said that their Dad was a wonderful chap and they looked forward to the day when they would be old enough to stand as committee members.

So Albert Docker set to work and produced, with the minimum of delay, a design to make the old pier impregnable. The idea was to encase the structure completely in india rubber tyres. As a prophylactic measure, this design would doubtless have stopped boats bonking the pier. But the Council felt, quite rightly that they didn't want their pier looking like an inflated Tate Gallery art exhibit.

Docker's next design showed flair, if not practicality, and that was to dismantle and re-build the whole pier on dry land. The site that Docker chose was Western Esplanade. The Council liked this idea, considering the amount of money that would be saved on maintenance: The paint: The barnacle proofing — that sort of thing.

However, a group of local environmentalists rather objected to this idea on the not unreasonable grounds they wouldn't have been able to take a stroll along the prom without some yobbo dropping his used chip packet (or worse) on top of them. Nor indeed, would ladies of refinement have been able to walk along the pier without some yobbo peering up their skirts.

It was getting all very controversial and the local environmental office was soon visited by a yobbo who declared that he wouldn't have been seen dead looking up a lot of stuffy ladies skirts. Not that there was much worth looking at, he added in a typical yobbo manner. This statement so scandalized one elderly environmentalist that he expired on the spot from an overheated imagination.

Fortunately, Albert Docker arrived at a plan that seemed to satisfy everybody. It worked like this. At the very end of the pier, way out to sea, a brand new *variety theatre* was built. This proved quite far enough for some, and the performances there by touring groups like 'The Fol De Rols' of Bradford kept people away in *droves.* The star turn, Norman "Cheeky Monkey" Sproule, was enough to ensure that no boat went anywhere *near* the pier for years. In fact, Southend Council was more than happy to subsidize the Fol De Rols and other acts like it if it meant that the precious pier was safe from attack.

This blissful state lasted for many years until, inevitably variety died, and not even Ten Pin Bowling or Space Invaders could hold back the shipping forecast.

And so the marauding merchantmen returned with a vengeance and began cutting the poor old pier down to size again.

Even the fun-loving Luftwaffe got into the act during World War Two by dropping parachute mines as a holiday treat. But the pier was much too hotly defended by the Navy who responded by blasting off with something far more deadly. As a result many German aircraft limped home with sticks of Southend rock peppering their fueslages. Later, an outbreak of dental decay was reported amongst the Luftwaffe pilots, thus shortening the war by a few days.

History aside,things are now definitely on the down-turn again and it has been reported that Southend Council are, even now, on the lookout for any likely ideas to prevent the total demolition of the pier.

One option has been to fully re-wire Peter Pan's Playground and bring back the fairy lights. This was objected to by Gay Lib for no particular reason. Councillor Wayne Docker then proposed the novel idea of shifting Southend lock, stock and winkle over to Tenerife. His idea was overruled when it was discovered that he owned a large plot of land at Los Cristianos.

Other ideas have surfaced but none have been really worthy of much consideration. But don't be put off. Southend welcomes any practical scheme and it could make you a fortune in pier railway tickets. But please hurry! The omens are not good. You see, I wouldn't be at all surprised if the tide was now on the turn and the next, and possibly fatal collision with Southend Pier wasn't due any minute . . . now!

Tall Limericks of Essex

The thing I find shocking
about people in Bocking
is that none of them
laughs at a joke.
So I would suggest
(If you'll forgive me my jest)
what they need is a
jolly good poke!

No. 8 The Most Life-Like Ventriloquist's Dummy In Essex

OWNED by magician Arthur Ashton, seen here performing alfresco in Basildon town centre. The most life-like ventriloquist's dummy in Essex is called 'Lord Cecil' and is seen here in this photograph (we think!)

No. 9 The Tiniest Corn Dolly In Essex

THIS was made by Mrs Julia Stone of Hockley in Essex. She is seen here showing it off to the camera. Also showing it off to the camera is daughter, Angela.

Grave Concerns

A REAL growth-area in the county of Essex (apart, that is from lots of lovely new traffic lights in Chelmsford) is archaeology. Ancient history is literally beneath our twinkling toes. Old bits of the past whether in the form of Roman villas, Viking graveyards, or perhaps the charred remains of some Neolithic Planning Office. All these and more await the questing trowel; the light flick of the sable-haired brush.

In fact, Essex has always been a favourite region to bury things in. For example, the extremely ancient site of Chelmsford was used by Danish settlers as a rubbish dump. This dump remained until the Romans moved in, and this is the reason why Chelmsford in one. (A Roman town that is.)

In 1083 AD, the infamous Duke of Ongar (see Edward's Potato Machine) used the nearby hamlet of Fyfield to bury all his ex-wives. This measure caused a local outcry at the time, particularly from all his ex-wives who just happened to be very much *alive* at the time of burial.

Present day archaeologists are very keen to trace as many of these old burial sites as possible, if only to secure their employment prospects. A study of the names of villages and towns can provide useful clues as to where some of these burial sites are. Scholars have placed particular emphasis on places with the suffix, 'FIELD'.

For example, *BroomFIELD.*

This name was thought, for many years to have derived from the old Norse word 'Bronfeld' which means, 'My pigs have run away. My wife has run away and I am all alone. I wish my pigs would come back!' In fact, this is erroneous. The name Broomfield originated in 632 AD due to the accidental uncovering of a quantity of Witches Sticks in a meadow. The sticks were hastily covered up again when it was discovered that Halloween night was not far off.

Great BardFIELD. (Originally West Dumpton).

The name was changed when in 1616 a huge cartload of the collected works of William Shakespeare was ceremoniously buried by outraged members of the BRING BACK BACON COMMITTEE. The headquarters of this committee was in Dunmow, but just *why* they went to West Dumpton remains a mystery.

WethersFIELD

The local iron-age farmers and horticulturalists were getting a bit fed up with the predictions of the resident meteorologist Neddy McCaskill. On one particularly stormy day, (after Neddy had forecast sunshine) they dragged him from his hovel, frog-marched him to a nearby fen and buried him up to his neck in warm peat. There he was left to rot. Later he was turned into solid-fuel brickettes and sold at the market to ward off hypothermia, especially in the summer-time.

FinchingFIELD.

A much photographed place and used as a location for television commercials advertising things like 'real' country margarine. Although Finchingfield is a renowned beauty spot, it wasn't always like that. Rumour has it that in 953 AD all the ugly people in the village were rounded up and garotted, or to use the old term, 'Finched'. The bodies were then laid to rest under a vast mound of old calendars, just off the B1057.

BradFIELD

This pretty village was originally called *Bard*field, but thanks to an illiterate and dyslexic map maker of Ongar (which used to be called *Ronga,* thanks to the illiterate and dyslexic map maker of Ongar (or Ronga) who transposed the 'R'), the name stuck. The illiterate and dyslexic map-maker of Ongar was stuck too, about ten feet underground, put there by a mob of irrate Bradfield villagers who were narked about their mail always going astray.

Which brings us to the *End,* or places that end in *End,* (not to be confused with *Pratt's Bottom* which is another county altogether.

Howlett END.

This hamlet got lumbered with *this* name from our merry Ongar map chap. An 'L' crept in and, as this writer can attest, it can be a right pain in the end.

Bacon END.

Where in 1617, the BRING BACK SHAKESPEARE COMMITTEE ceremoniously buried members of the BRING BACK BACON COMMITTEE. (See Great Bardfield.)

Church END.

Something of a curiosity, for there are *two* Church Ends in Essex. Even more curious, archaeologists have failed to find any church remains at either place. Archivists have speculated on the singular aspect of this. They have reached the conclusion that it all has something to do with a 14th century priest called Beazley. Records show that Beazley was an alchemist. Coupled with his interest in natural science and astronomy, it is conceivable that he stumbled upon the formula for some sort of powerful explosive. This may explain why the two Church Ends are separated by twenty miles (look it up). If he was experimenting in his church at the time of an explosion, this would account for the lack of any remains.

Beazley END. (Ten miles *east* of Church End)

The probable landing site for the body of Beazley.

Ford END.

Nothing to do with water. In fact Ford is a corruption of 'fiord'. It was in 1023 AD that an Essex nobleman called Adric Waterhouse visited Norway for a holiday and went for a float down Sognefiord. He was so impressed by the wonder of his trip that he decided to recreate a Norwegian fiord in Essex. Of course, it was only going to be a *half-size* scale model, but even so, the task was a daunting one.

Adric chose a site for his fiord (just north of Chelmsford) and began excavations (with a little help from two thousand serfs) and within a year a huge gully had been cut with earth piled up on each side to form 'mountains'. Well satisfied, Adric ordered

that the gully be filled with water and the ends sealed. When all was complete, Adric embarked down the centre of his fiord in a boat, whereupon the earth 'mountains' collapsed inwards and buried the hapless Adric in the biggest mud bath in Essex. It is not reported what Adric said at the time although the two thousand serfs had an apposite word for him.

But what of recent times? Are there burial sites in the making? I would contend that there are. I would argue that one has only to look at the results of something called THE ESSEX PLAN. It's a form of system building which has taken off in a big way. Such is the pressure on space and the high cost of land that whole communities are now buried vertically and above ground. The very best example of this building technique can be seen near the River Crouch. Unfortunately, people who go to this area are never heard from again. The place that I am referring to is, of course, South Woodham Ferrers.

No. 10 The Least Successful Pop Group In Essex

NAMED 'The Writtles', John, Paul and Morris McKenzie toured all over Essex (looking for somewhere to play) in the late nineteen sixties. Their only recording, 'We belong to Chignall Smealy' was once played on Radio Caroline during a power failure which put the station off the air.

No. 11 The Most Non-Haunted House In Essex

THE owner of Mundon Lodge, Mr. Clive Terling has for many years failed to attract the 'right kind' (as he puts it) of ghost. Mr. Terling would be the first to admit that he's a spook racist. "Only the *white* sort will do here," he says, "And they must have been born and buried in Essex with plenty of well-bred moans and groans. None of your imported stuff thank you very much!"

Part of Mr. Terling's problem is the state of repair of his property. One ghost recently confessed that he wouldn't be seen dead in a place like that!

Boris The Radio Pioneer

THE renaissance of radio broadcasting in recent years has led to a proliferation of local channels, of which one of the latest is 'Countywide' BBC Essex.

Now, the received wisdom is that 'wireless telephony' became what we understand as 'radio broadcasting' on June the 15th 1920, when the famous Australian singer, Nellie Melba broadcast a special concert of songs (including Home Sweet Home and the first stanza of God Save The King) from an experimental studio in Chelmsford. The concert was commissioned by the Marconi Company and was heard by a rapt audience of enthusiasts (at least for radio broadcasting) all over the world. The signal is reported to have been received anything up to 2,000 miles away. The story that Miss Melba thought she had to climb the aerial and *shout* is apocryphal.

By February 1922, the Marconi Company were transmitting concerts on a weekly basis from a hut at their Writtle works, (that hut still exists and it is lodged in the grounds of Chelmsford's Kings Road Junior School.) In November of that same year, the British Broadcasting Company was formed under the directorship of John Reith.

However, I've now discovered evidence that the county of Essex spawned a radio station that pre-dates the original Marconi broadcast.

It was in June of 1919, that an ex-wartime navy signals officer called Boris Bertram Charlesworth set up a modest transmitter and studio and began broadcasting from the top of a disused water-tower in Rainsford Road. Charlesworth christened his station 'Wireless Chelmsford' (which could also claim to be the first *pirate* radio station as it was unlicenced) and he equipped it with a collection of redundant war department apparatus which

he financed with his not insubstantial gratuity.

Although primitive by modern standards, the studio and transmitter performed satisfactorily, even if Charlesworth didn't. For the unfortunate fact was that Boris Charlesworth had a gigantic and festering *chip* on his shoulder. The exact reasons for all this are unclear, but it would appear that his wartime experiences plus a lack of promotion and a blighted love affair (well you know what sailors are) all contributed to his instability, irascibility, and general utter hatred of mankind.

This, in turn, reflected upon the programmes (or *programme*, for there *was* only one) that Charlesworth inflicted upon the hapless inhabitants of Essex. It transpired that the first radio programme in the world was also the *worst* radio programme in the world. (At least at the time of writing.)

This seminal transmission consisted of nothing more and nothing less than a particularly crackly gramophone recording of 'The Laughing Policeman' which was played *backwards* and at *half* speed. This aural agony was repeated every two minutes for hours at a stretch.

Charlesworth had designed this deleterious cacophony in the hope of scuttling the *very idea* of broadcasting forever. He reasoned, that if people heard his programme, they would become so nauseated that they would abandon radio for all time. As a consequence they would be forced into an existance of *total boredom* of an evening. Doing the sort of things we all try to avoid, like talking to one another, joining in things, doing a bit of decorating and being generally sociable.

It almost worked.

However, this dastardly scheme to strangle the infant radio in what amounted to wireless cot-death, failed totally on three important counts.

Firstly: Just about nobody in Essex in 1919 *had* a radio set upon which to receive the signal.

Secondly: The very *last* place to contemplate installing electrical equipment is in a *water* tower.

And thirdly: Well, it goes without saying that Charlesworth

soon electrocuted himself when making a fatal circuit between his finger, the gramophone needle and a live thermionic valve. Unfortunately, he wasn't wearing welly boots at the time.

With the studio off the air for good, the dire intentions, aims and objectives of Boris Charlesworth died with him. At least for a short while, for just around the corner in November of 1922 the world famous BBC (or Boris Bertram Charlesworth for short) started broadcasting 'The Laughing Policeman' all over again.

This sent people into paroxysms of delight at the prospect of really interesting evenings ahead. They now, no longer had to face the appalling prospect of having to talk to one another, join in things, stick up wall-paper or kick the cat.

Even with Boris Charlesworth now long gone, the irony is that his programme standards appear to live on. His legacy is still heard on a daily basis throughout the world. Take, for example the uncanny resemblance that *Radio Albania* has to Wireless Chelmsford, or for that matter Radio One.

But it's perhaps as well to reflect that *true* pioneers are always ahead of their time. As history has shown, Boris Charlesworth may have been a bit off his dial, but he was never really out of tune. In fact some people consider that he was the cat's whiskers.

Tall Limericks of Essex

Never disparage Harwich
It's delights are for all
to see.
But avoid getting locked out of
Parkeston
Unless you can find the quay.

A man from Southend
went right round the bend.
his relations from Leigh
didn't invite him for tea.
Instead they departed
for places uncharted.
Like Brightlingsea.

Solution to Spot The Essex Difference

In fact there *is* no difference in the two pictures. Each is identical. However, if you *found* some differences then this could mean two things. Firstly, you're an incorrigible cheat. Shame on you! And secondly, you've obviously lived far too long in Essex. As a consequence you are suffering from fantasy delusions of the worst kind. Take a job at the Essex Planning Authority immediately!

No. 12 The Most Unorthodox Vicar In Essex

THE Rev. Roger Middleton of Great Henny (seen here in typical garb with wife Marion) would promote christianity by putting 'the fear of God' (as he called it) into his parishioners. He and his wife would crouch behind grave stones at night in his church yard and leap out suddenly at people as they passed by. Not unnaturally, some people passed *on* which tended to increase the congregation, if only in the grave yard.

The Tall Tales Guide to Essex Pets

A brief look at the more outstanding examples in the County.

No. One: The Tiptree Tabby

This is *Strawberry*, a famous mouser from Blackthorn Fruit Farm. *Strawberry* has personally exterminated 375 rats, 633 field mice, 98 voles, 13 rooks, 78 wood pigeons, 28 pheasants, 38 finches, 118 hedgehogs, 256 sparrows, 60 rabbits, 40 hamsters, 29 budgies, 15 dogs, 4 sheep, 3 cows, 2 paperboys and one milkman.

As Mr. Arthur Billet of Blackthorn Fruit Farm remarks, "That's the trouble with old Strawberry, he just doesn't know when to stop."

No. Two: The Clacton Cocker Spaniel

Cyril the cocker spaniel is owned by Mr. and Mrs. Walker of Bokings Close in Clacton. *Cyril* is a real boon to the Walkers'. He collects the newspaper each day, makes the tea, sweeps the lounge, re-wires the house and completes the income tax returns. Occasionally, if he feels like it, he'll give the car a 10,000 mile service.

Cyril was last seen writing comedy scripts for Radio Four and speeches for a prominent politician. *Cyril* likes to have Sundays off though.

No. Three: The Gosfield Goldfish

Bruce the goldfish is a renowned mimic. He can imitate any kind of fish you care to name. He once impersonated a piranha and it was so effective that *Bruce*'s owner, Mr. Clive Gittings is still recovering. However, Mr. Gittings' beautifully and intricately constructed metal hand tends to need a spot of oil from time to time. Mr. Gittings has considered boiling *Bruce* to extract the oil for his metal hand, assuming, of course, he can get anywhere near *Bruce*'s tank.

No. Four: The Basildon Bosom-O-Gram

Miss Samantha Seksism is quite well-known in the area of her vital statistics. She once posed in the nude for Henry Mogg. Henry Mogg was a bit surprised at the time as he was just walking home from work at the baked bean factory.

Samantha's Bosom-O-Gram service is much in demand. County Council committee meetings are always enlivened when Sam is in attendance. Says close friend Councillor Lionel Docker, "I've never seen her before in my life!"

Flying Down to Mersea Island

ABOUT twelve years ago, (October 1975 to be exact) it was reported in the *Essex Chronicle* that a group of school-boys spotted what they described as a large object hovering ninety feet above the ground and ablaze with lights.

This wondrous sight occurred at a place called Pollards Meadow in Springfield near Chelmsford. The boys, who were kicking a ball about at the time, were quite startled and one of them is reported as saying, "We thought it was going to come down and land right in the middle of our pitch!"

An understandable reaction in the circumstances. However, the strange object *didn't* land, but zoomed off soon after, quite as mysteriously as it had arrived.

This begs the obvious question as to just *what* the boys are supposed to have witnessed. Dismissing the frivolous prospect that the object was an aerial number 19 bus full of flying football fans, if the boys are to be believed, what they say they saw on that day was a Flying Saucer. Another term is Unidentified Flying Object, or UFO for short.

Although the boys had a good chance to observe details of this object, not a lot was gleaned from the sighting: The colour scheme, the number plate, what the driver looked like, that sort of thing. This is not at all unusual, for the human brain gets in a bit of a jumble when confronted with the truly peculiar. And there's nothing more truly peculiar than the subject of Flying Saucers, as we shall see.

In fact, flying saucers have been a bit out of the news of late. They were quite thick on the ground, (or I should say in the *air*) during the mid nineteen sixties. The whole country seemed awash with reports of space-ships from Venus. Not a day went by without some fantastic account of bright lights in the sky, loud bangs, funny smells, holes in roofs, dead cats and mind-numbing rays.

To some, this might seem quite normal, taking into account all the other things we have to put up with in this country. Some people even set up Flying Saucer Clubs and went out Sky Watching on lonely hills in order to gather evidence and make contact with beings from other worlds. All quite harmless and a bit of a giggle really.

Mersea Island had its fair share of UFO's and the local saucer club would often camp out in fields in the hope of making a 'sighting'. What that 'sighting' eventually turned out to be proved slightly unexpected if not confusingly unidentified.

Which brings us to Eric Shuttlewood. Now Eric was an East Mersea postman (not that it is at all relevant) and quite a down-to-earth sort of chap. It is fair to say that he didn't go a bundle on flying saucers, and *least* of all flying saucer clubs. To him, any one who joined such outfits was half way (if not *all* the way) to the Funny Farm, and he rather quaintly referred to these people as 'Saucer Sillies'.

Not content to leave sleeping Saucer Sillies to lie, Eric Shuttlewood determined to teach them all a 'lesson', as he put it, that they would never forget. It was also a lesson that *Eric* would never forget.

Eric had read somewhere that the flying saucer world was bedevilled by hoaxes. Fraudulent claims of contacts with Martians. Photographs of interstellar car hub-caps, and dentists professing to be Masters of the Universe. And yet, Eric noted, some people *believed* all that rubbish. Under these conditions, Eric gleefully reasoned *his* hoax could not fail, and he set about his preparations.

About a week later, Eric made his way to a field. It was late at night and the moon was full. Conditions were just perfect for what Eric had in mind. In the middle of this field, camped out complete with cameras, binoculars, UFO detectors and flasks of hot weak tea was the East Mersea branch of the International Sky Scouts Flying Saucer Spotting Club, as yet all unsuspecting.

Eric Shuttlewood crept silently into the field and positioned himself behind a gorse bush. Satisfying himself that he had not been spotted, he unloaded his bag and began assembling his hoax. This involved the use of a small, empty margarine tub, a candle, a large paper bag, some thread and a white lurex body stocking.

Now, in case you're wondering just what sort of depraved hoax this was going to be, let me apprise you of the situation.

The small margarine tub was placed on the ground and the candle fixed into it. The thread was then attached to the tub and the paper bag in the manner of a parachute. The candle was then lit and the warm air caused the paperbag to expand. When sufficient heat had been generated, up went the entire contraption, into the air, bobbing and darting about just like (yes, you guessed it) a flying saucer!

But what about that white lurex body-stocking, I hear you cry? Well, Eric Shuttlewood was actually *wearing* that, plus a smattering of his wife's make-up. It was all designed to give him an unearthly appearance. Just the job to startle a susceptible saucer seeker!

Eric watched as his home-made 'saucer' wobbled across the sky, right over to where the Sky Scouts were sitting. If things had gone according to plan, this is what *should* have happened next. With the attention of the UFO spotters firmly fixed on the flying paper bag, Eric was going to leap wildly into the field, make some WHOO! WHOO! noises, act like a Martian and then scarper sharpish before his ruse was rumbled.

Unfortunately, things started to go wrong when the still night air suddenly took it upon itself to create an eddy. This caused the drifting 'saucer' to change direction, straight back to where the lurex attired Eric was hiding. The candle in its little tub spluttered and spat a bit of flame up to the paper bag. Suddenly, the entire construction caught alight and dropped with a fiery and quite spectacular flash right on top of the startled Eric Shuttlewood. Flames licked at the lurex body-stocking, causing it to melt in painful patches and causing Eric to utter agonizing ARGH! ARGH'S! in place of the WHOO! WHOO'S!

Watched by the bemused saucer spotters, Eric staggered about in circles, beating himself frantically in order to put the flames out. In desperation, he finally ripped off the charred lurex suit and rolled around quite naked in the damp grass. His pitiful moans and groans sounded, at the very least, totally unlike a Martian.

A passing police patrol car drove up at that precise moment and with some haste Eric Shuttlewood was led away under a coat, protesting his innocence and trying to explain to the police officers that he really *wasn't* a transvestite nudist arsonist!

The incident was later reported in the press, so naturally things got even *more* confused. For example, one UFO spotter swore blind that Eric Shuttlewood had, in fact, flown over his head in a giant pink pudding basin, bellowing in a raucous voice, "Hello, I'm from Mars you morons!"

This was contradicted by another who maintained that Eric popped out of the ground and threw a snowball at him. Another person claimed that Eric was in fact Jesus on his way (via East Mersea) to Jerusalem. A lady saucer hunter (who wished to remain anonymous) said that Eric was definitely cigar shaped.

Just *which* part of Eric she was referring to isn't clear. But it seems that the *only* thing that *was* clear was that nobody was really clear about anything that happened that night.

The Mersea police, on the other hand were in *no* doubt that they had a clear lunatic on their hands. Eric Shuttlewood was eventually released with a fine and told to keep the peace, but he had to abandon his career as a postman due to the constant snide remarks about *air*mail letters and, "Bit late today, John. What happened, did your flying saucer get a *puncture?*"

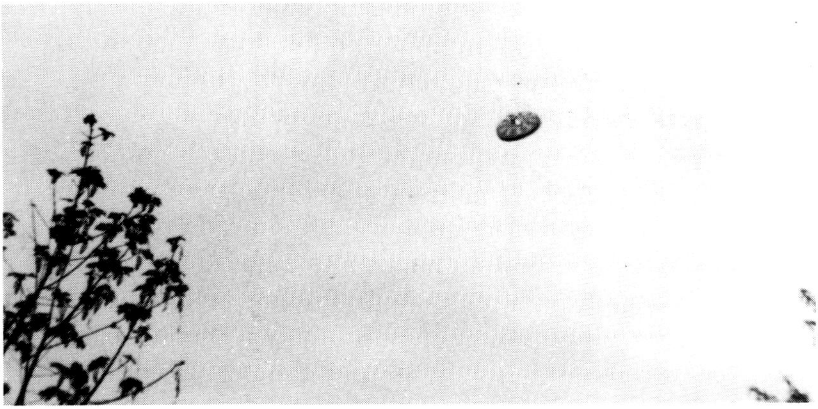

An extremely clear photograph of a dust-bin lid. What is not so clear is why a dust-bin lid was flying over Mersea Island in the first place. This has since been dismissed as an optical illusion.

Eric Shuttlewood has vanished into obscurity, but flying saucers are still reported, zipping about the skies. So remember, things are not *always* what they seem. The next time you see something strange in the sky, consider this. It could very well be somebody just like you or me, flying a *kite.*